Another side of me
REVISITED

By

Lawrence Douglas Davis

SONGS

Illustrated

Dedication

This book is dedicated to the poets, the thinkers and most of all to the dreamers. To those who look at the world and wonder. To those who look inside themselves and delve deep into their inmost fears and their greatest loves, and to those who just like to put words to paper.

We are dreamers all.

Especially to my wife, who fills my life with joy.

by the same author

Another side of me (first version)
A book of poems.

Demons and Things
An illustrated book of children's poems
and short tales.

INSIGHTS on how to draw the human figure and
characterisation.
Instructional drawing book
suitable for 12 - 112-year-olds.

DoublemanArt
Artwork by the author

INDEX

Introduction

Letters, symbols of our age that convert the spoken word into print. Words transform us, take us to another realm, to a place of dreams or into our darkest thoughts laid bare. What we cannot say out loud we speak to outsiders with print as we communicate our innermost feelings and in doing so, we try to gain an insight, not only to ourselves, but to the wider world around

Songs of WAR

The Call

I wander through the news reels so full of hate and rage,
how did we ever get here how did we reach this stage?
Some names are ever present some slither to the past,
some names remain forever and some they never last.
The *Calls* the same, it never
changes, some *Calls* are built to last,
all forever cast their shadow,
shadows from the past.
Why do we hate?
What takes us there?
What makes the past so up to date,
What makes us want this hate?
Kingdoms come and kingdoms go
But the *Call* was built to last.
Let's gather round my bonny lads,
So, we can turn the present
into the present past.
You hear it now that ancient *Call*
It summons you to war
Let's take the present, my bonny lads,
Let's take it to the past.
The *Call*, the *Call*, that ancient *Call.*
Echoes built to last.

Kingdoms come and Kingdoms go,
But the *Call* was built to last.

Flanders 1

Somewhere on a dark and misty night
A lonely figure stumbles to the fight.
He is lost, alone and cold,
No friend to trust, no friend to hold.
On a Flanders field the moon shines down
And paints a nightmare on this ground.
The green of home that he once knew
Are lost amidst the deafening dew
And his wish is death will pass him by.
For him the nights are judgements call
The Last of days, the final call.
The mist rolls down these hundred years
Across a field that's filled with tears
Yet still he walks this Tommy true
He walks them all for me and you.
No rest for him this gallant lad
Doomed to walk the misty night
The curse of war, the eternal fight
Humanities curse upon us all
Until, until the guns are still.

Flanders 2

In a Flanders field you can see them grow
One by one, in a row
A cold and calm earthly red
There to honour the passing dead
The years have flown
Time gone by
Yet still the poppies seem to cry
The crimson red, the silent night
When Britain's youth rushed to the fight
A field of red, a tear to shed,
Lest we forget the fallen dead.

2022

War, it came to our door
You can't hide
You can't hide
You can't run anymore.
Rivers of rain
A stench in the air
And death rides around
As blood, the blood it runs freely
Soaks into the ground.
Screams of the children
Cries of the old
The young they die fast
While the brave, they die bold
But they die just the same
Their stories untold.
The sky darkens over
The clouds coloured red
No birds fly above
For they dine on the dead.
White bones upon the grass
Clothing tattered and torn
No more the brave soldier
For the soldiers are no more.
When it's all over
Who stands the victor?
Who counts the loss?
For war is war
And it comes at a cost.

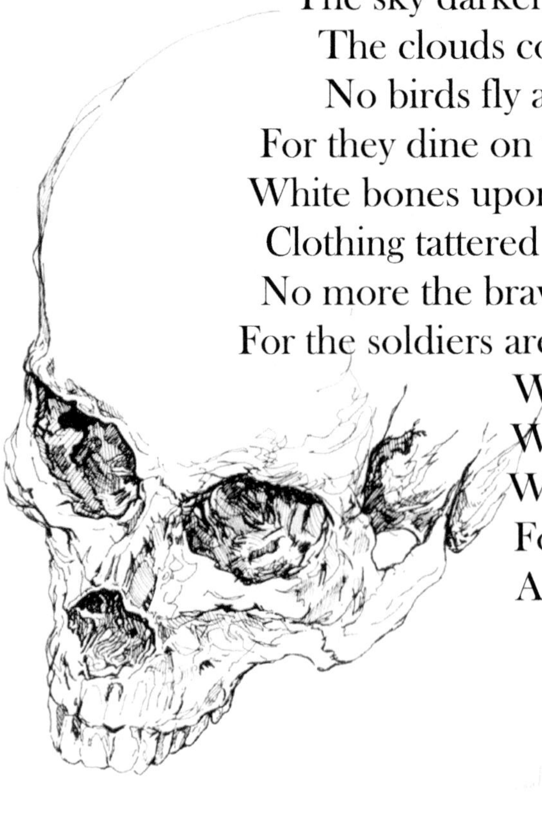

Don't talk

Don't talk to me of brotherhood!
Don't talk to me of pain
Your words are full of barbarism
And your words are all the same.
If you are religion
I will not hear your name.

For religion is a sword
That cuts the human heart
In the name of your one God
To strike my soul apart.
For religion raises man above the cattle
Then casts him low like swine
And there amongst the mud and filth
Leaves him there to dine.

So, I pray to the Gods I don't believe in
To free me from this shit
And hope that one God hears me
If only for a bit.

Free us from your chains
Give us back our voice
For we can be much more than this
If we only had a choice.

Old rubber boat

We once set sail in an old rubber boat,
It didn't quite sink, yet it didn't quite float.
It mingled; it straddled, in a halfway float,
The day we set sail in an old rubber boat.
We made our way to a fort in the Solent
It was a daredevil day; it was a daredevil moment.
We passed the odd buoy, the red flashing light,
A guide in the darkness
On a cold winters night.
The taste of freedom, like salt in the air
Desperation, desperation,
Too many in an old rubber boat,
But desperation, desperation,
Kept that old boat afloat.
Are we wanted?
Are we needed?
Is freedom a joke?
Do we suffer the trolls and the old racist yoke?
The waves they went up
The waves they went down
Sometimes they twisted that old boat around.
The whiteness of foam on a dark winters' night,
Screams of the children, ghosts of despair
Embraced one another like spray in the air.
Then land, that suddenly springs into view
Land of the free, for me, or for you?
We just want to live
We just want to be free.

What's next / BLM

The sky, a sweet and mellow blue
A cloudless sky
A blameless sky
To carry this day through.
Yet wait!
I hear a cry which beckons me to stare
But what my eyes do look upon
Wish not to tarry there.
This scene, this man-made hell
This yoke that drags me down
Race and colour beat's its drum
And marches into town.
Brothers, sisters, both black and white
Their bodies drawn into the night
Their hopes and dreams now fade away
On this, a torrid, wretched day.
The grip of fear
The boot, the heel
The gun, the smoke, the pepper spray
Walk hand in hand with death today.

Listen!
Do you hear the call!
That carries all into this war.
Put down the sword
Lift up the pen
So, we can try to start again.
A simple wish I'd like to keep
But decades stand on corpse's deep.

Songs of LOVE

Killer

She was a killer
Murder in her heart
Torture in her soul
She took me to the highest peak
And then she let me go.

Angels

Angels watching over us
They sometimes fall asleep
And then the heavens open
As Angels start to weep

Dance with me

Dance with me
Dance me on and on
Dance me to the end of love
Until all the stars are gone

The question

When I say I love you,
Do I mean it?
When you say you love me,
Is there anything to it?

When does love become an entity,
When does love take form?

Is it a hand that holds,
Or the look inside your eye?
Is it a touch,
Or in your last goodbye?

When is love real?
When does love begin?
Is love the final answer?
Or is love the greatest sin?

Camera

I clicked the camera this morning
I caught you with my eyes
The lens it floated to your body
Captured by your thighs.
I focused on you this morning
So soft, so gentle and pure
There I caught you
There I had you
So, I clicked the camera once more.
Our love will burn in the morning
And flow throughout the day
At night the angels will watch over us
So, our love won't fade away.

Narrow lanes

Narrow lanes and walkways
Lead to unknown paths
I will talk to you of dreams
And sing of rainbows new
And try to make you laugh again
For your smiles, they are few.

Narrow lanes and tiny walkways,
We walk to find the truth,
The wisdom in old age
Or the folly of our youth?

In dreams I call your name
And the words will kiss my lips.

Was I

Was I always such a dreamer
Did I ever play my part
Was I such a schemer
A dreamer without a start
Did I talk the talk
Not walk the walk
Did my dreams all fall apart?

Do I berate myself
Condemn myself
Was I such a foolish heart?

Here lays the key,
Do I believe in me?
Question, question
Two sides
One coin
Two sides to play their part
If I came through
If I came true...
I will always believe in you.

Hearts song

A song from the heart,
Do you have one?

Why? you ask me.

Every heart has a song, I say.

Some have many songs,
Some are sad and some reflective
But most are happy songs.
Childhood memories
Of long-lost friendships
Playing games
Or your first love,
Something that changed you into who you are today.
We all have songs.

You just need to remember the tune.

Drift

Shall I devour you in the darkness
In the silence of the night
As we merge into the oneness
In our sexual delight
Or will you come to me at sunrise
Just before the dawn
That sleepy moment
Waking moment
When we hold each other tight.
Will reality match our dreams
Or fade in life's daylight.

Is this the curse?
Loves burning heart
That tremulous step that faulters
As worlds do fall apart.

So, hold me close to midnight
Take my hand once more
Show me that you mean it
As I drift through heaven's door.

Broken windows

No one told me dreams were made of glass
No one said that dreams will never last
Look! see me in that dream
In a hazy floating light
Neither is it day, yet neither is it night.
Our love, our love as old as time
Come dream with me
Dream the dream sublime.
Our warmth, our heat, our bodies meet
Our legs and arms entwine.
Gossamer skin so smooth and clean
The velvet, with a wispy touch
As I probe the pleasures deep
Aroma's rise from bodies hot
From the body heat.
Sweet sensations and so the pleasure grows
A shudder, a rise, emotions unconstrained
Emotions we both share, entwine me in your thoughts
And in those thoughts release me
Freedom of the soul
Our bodies in the act of love
Have made my body whole.

And then...just then...I awaken
Gone the dream once more,
As I look down my dream lays there...
shattered on the floor.

Words

Do I hide the stranger
The one inside my head
His silent thoughts surround me
Words that go unsaid.

Words, they are the nearness in the night
Thoughts built into nightmares
Thoughts that bind me tight,
For words are wrought from passion
And words can do so many things,
Words keep me to you.

Sticks and stones can hurt me
But words are weapons too
Words can cut me deeper
Words as cool as ice
Words can have a coldness
A blade to pierce the heart
Words can leave me walking
But I'm dead right from the start

So, choose your words most carefully
Think of all the good they do
Words of love
Words of joy
Words of compassion and hope
Words are the torch, the light
That guide me home to you.
Words, more powerful than you can imagine
Just...words...

Laughter

See the children how they run, how they play,
how the sun fills the sky and brightens their day
with their laughter, that pushes the dark clouds away.
Rains not allowed, not in their sunny day.

I remember those days,
Not all you see,
But I remember the ones that mattered to me.
I'd watch my children begin to crawl
Then stand on two feet
Stand straight, stand tall.
I watched the look within their eyes,
A look of pride,
A look of surprise.
I'd see the summers
The winters
The spring
I'd listen for laughter that each year would bring.
They say the best things in life are free
Like love or sex
But it's laughter for me.
For laughter is love
Laughter sings life
Yes, laughter is the thing that I like the most
It's like strawberry jam on a warm piece of toast.

Love

Love, that old tale.
A tale so old it weaves like silken thread,
Weaving its way through time.
Love from the past
Love from the now and then
Love that never has an end.
Love that's consumed by hate
Love that's lost in cold debate
Love that buries itself so deep
Love that bursts and hearts do weep
Love intangible
Love twisted black like tarred old string
And love the poets wish to sing
Love, the sweet
Love, the strong
Love that ends when things go wrong.

Love, such a cruel and restless thing.

Love is

Love is such a silent feeling
Love is such a quiet beast
Its heart beats like thunder
Love brings passion to the feast.
It holds you tight in unseen chains
Shackles to bind your heart
Love, love can tear that heart apart.
Love is something poets dream of
Love is born up in the stars
Love is all that we embrace
Love is everyman's desire
Love can be written on your face.
Love is strong
Love is weak
Yet for love, we'd move a mountain
Love is something that we seek.
Love is found in tiny places
Love sings a silent song
Love whispers love
When everything goes wrong.

Love is...

OUT

When I go out
Just make me laugh
Say something funny
Don't let me go grouchy, grumbly and old
Bring me life
Let the laughter unfold.
At the end of it all
Fill me with gladness
Fill me with joy
Be un-PC for I'm only a boy.
I want laughter like heroin
So fix me a line
Fade me into bliss
For this is my time.
Just hold close my hand
Feel the life ebb away
And know I hold love
Forever today.
For love is more than just a shake of a hand
In that...
let it stand.

Don't forget to tell me a joke.

Songs of REFLECTION

A Covid perambulation

I went out walking as merrily as could be
Where I met a man in the street
Who sneezed all over me.
And then he coughed, a cough quite loud
And looking up – eyes above a tut,
Cursed the Gods above,
For this fine chap as he walked away
I could find I had no love.

I then went into a shop,
I tried to do my part.
I saw the signs and arrows
And kept six feet apart.
A lady came and trolleyed past
Going the opposite way
She looked at me and me at her
I think the kind of look I got
Kind of made her day.

And now the days have grown short
The nights blend into one
I feel the shadow creeping over me
It seems my time has come.
Too late for me to wear the mask,
Trapped inside a wooden cask.

Words of wisdom?

Words of wisdom
Whence do they come
From me, from you, from anyone?
Each person a prophet
Each word divine
Your words or His
Or maybe mine?
Truth and lies are they the same
As life begets death's merry game.

Find that love that holds your heart
Each beat
Each skip
Each one the start.

Keep your peace
Voice not your fears
Hold your hand
Hold close your tears.
Keep your faith
Hold your path
Don't look back
Forget the past
The past was never meant to last.

Faces

I passed myself in a mirror today
Not sure who I saw
I had to go back and look again
Pulled a few faces
Stupid really, childish.
I stopped
I looked again
It's in the eyes, I suppose.
We don't really look people straight in the eyes.
Today, I looked into mine.
I'm not sure who was there
For we wear so many faces
The past is gone
But there, right there, in the past,
I wore many, many faces.
Today that face has changed again...
I've grown into it
The lines
The grey hair
But the mind is as it always was
Childish, uncomprehending, forgetful
Drifting into dreaming
And so, I look once more.
I am that face
The face that I wear now
This face
This one
I hope and pray that it fits.

Son
SCHOOLBOY
STUDENT
Worker
LOVER
Husband
Father
ARTIST
Author
OAP
Grandad

Life

When I was a child
I drew like a child.
It wasn't that I didn't see the real world,
I saw a child's world.
If I drew a house, it was square,
The windows were square
Then I'd place a cross inside them
And hey presto! A window.
The door would be a box
And the roof a triangle,
Even if I didn't know what a triangle was.
It was simple
It was easy
Now, now I procrastinate
I ponder
I wonder
Is this real?
Does it look like it should?
Drawing is now...complicated

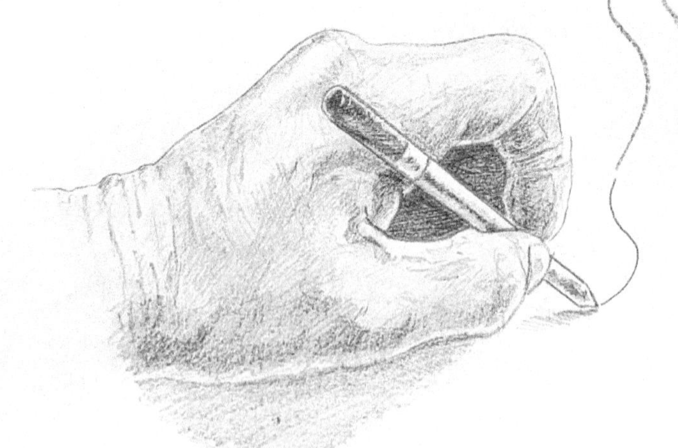

I've grown old.

Old man's lament

The grey it floats above me, it hovers around my ears
It shouts!
It yells!
It screams of passing years.
What folly brought me here
As deity's do ask,
'*What sin was born in me,*
For the ravages of time
To come and visit thee?'

Wake not the gods,
Busy in their slumbers.
Count the days,
Not the numbers.

Dreamer

Look into the mirror
Pray tell me what I see
What strangers face
What countenance
Looks straight back at me.

Vanities of the heart
Ego like a fire
Eyes grown dim with age
No longer flame desire.

Skin now crossed with decades lines
Their blemished tracks race here and there
Youth and spirit, now all is lost
Old bones grown weak at such a cost.
Ambition quelled with passing time
But how I've loved this life of mine.

Life, true love
That beating heart
As dreams now fade from view
But every dream this dreamer dreams
Brings me back to you.

Old fears

I hear it now, bumps in the night
That quickening pace, a step unseen.
It's faster now, such speed, it flies
Old fears grow new
Old fears revived.

The paralysis
It soon takes hold
But courage, courage now
A thing I must unfold.
So, I steel myself
My manly dome
But fear is here
It has come home.
So many steps, to and fro
It seems he knows not where to go.

No more the creak upon the stair
No breath I hear that lingers there
And yet the sound persists
I hear it clear
That booming beat inside my ear.
The wife, she turns and melts away
To dream a dream another day.
The sweat, the noise, now subsides
The pounding less, the noise abates
No creak of handle, no creak of hinge
Silence reigns
Still the door
As the quiet night returns once more.

Your age or mine

There's a time to be young.
There's a time to be old.
Well, that's what I've heard.
That's what I've been told.
The first flush of youth
That first taste of love
As the hormones give chase.
Loves first go at love, loves own rat race.
Love's first try at sex
Never knowing what's right
Or what to do next.
Why do we try to hunt love down?
Why do we scrabble, seeking love that's true
But scrabble it seems is a thing that we do.
And when children appear
Love comes once again
For a child we hold dear.
Then suddenly, in the wink of an eye
The nest has been flown
How the time has gone by.
This body that once held the blossom of youth
Has grown old it seems
Long in the tooth.
Not quite so nimble
No rushing to bed
The passions of youth
Just a dream in my head.
Old age is not so bad,
Well, that's what I've heard.
That's what I've been told.
Whoever said that,
Wasn't that old.

Do they get up at night
And go for a piss?
Wonder if the pan is a hit or a miss.
Do they forget things like the time of the day
And nobody calls to come out to play.
I wonder when life turns into a blur
Will I know if I miss it?
Why worry I say of things yet to be
So, I take time for a biscuit
And a nice cup of tea.

In the midnight

I wonder when he'll stalk me
As I lay upon my bed
That faceless shadow
The one we know as Death.

Will I hear his creepy footsteps
Click-clack across the floor
Or is it just the midnight
And the creaking of a door?
I've seen him dance before me
Numerous as I recall,
Twinkle, twinkle...
A life that is no more.

So, I lay here in the midnight
And watch the passage of my breath
Listen to the darkness
For the one we know as Death.
What colours will he bring me
As he sits upon my chest
What music will he feed me
That sweet silent song of death.

Quiet place

Picture this, a quiet place
A field that holds no human trace
The grass a glowing emerald green
Could such a place have ever been?
A world where no one stomps around
And the only thing to kiss the ground
Is the gentle rain that trickles down.

But now the rain has gone away
The sky is clear for this new day.
This day begins, not in gentle breeze
But claps of thunder, of man's decease.
The earth so pure in her maiden's delight
Is rent with cries that split the night.
The grass is gone.
The sky, a bloody red.
The sea turned black; the fish are dead.
Only fool's wait to see
Could it
Can it
Truly be?

Stop the world, hold back this scene
Take me too where I had been
Pass me quick for pity's sake
Least my soul is sure to break.
Take me to that quiet place
To azure blue and emerald green,
Could such a place have ever been?

I watch

I watch
I see it
I see that time runs but one way
And that on such a pretty face
Time has left its mark
I see the shadow as it passes by
That flickering light
The memories
The smiles
And laughter too
I'll always see your face so true
Those eyes that shine
They gleamed like stars
So, I watch, and I watch
I see it
I hear the tick
I hear the tock
Life goes on, that endless clock
I love you true
I always will
Until the clock of time stands still.

Marble

Do not paint me with the colours of the rainbow
For I am as prepossessed of greys as the next man.
What strength I have
Is granted only in the eye of the beholder
For the eye sees only what it wants to see.
So, breathe,
Take shelter in a breath
And stand me not upon marble
As I am balanced on unsteady feet.
I am full to the brim with human failings
I possess not the wisdom of the gods
Nor do I hold a cup of endless charity.
I fall endlessly, but hide each trip.
I can be no more
I am me
I am you
We are the same.

I had to

I had to be the hero
I had to be the one
A fool with foolish schemes
A player in my dreams.

I had to be the one
To travel to the top
Then down into the pit
I had to chase the light
To get the final hit.

I had to comfort rage
And sooth away my hate
I had to quench my lust
Before I faced my fate.

I've had to do so many things
Many words have passed my lips
The bearer of ill tidings
A tongue with razor tips.

I had to look through many windows
To see what's in or out
To hear the children crying
To hear all mother's shout
I had to look
I had to see
I've had to chase the years
To find the one true me.

Angel's lament

They are here now like knights of old
With harrowing stories to unfold.
They have your song
Those clapping hands
The rattle of steel from old saucepans.
The trumpets blow, the bugles loud
They rally around as the numbers grow
Those angels of the NHS
Are people, just like all the rest.

But when the dragon meets its end
And normal times return once more
Like slumbering giants, they're at the door.
The screams, the cries, the old abuse
The publics pride has lost its use.
No calls to give them high born praise
Now that we have normal days.
The old refrains take rise,
The punches and spit into an Angel's eyes.
The fear, the stress is home again.
Once Britain's pride, hero's true,
Are the jokers in the pack
The beasts have returned
The venom has come back.
They risked it all, each day and night
Stood their ground
Did not take flight
And as the numbers begin to fall
No more the clapping at the door.
Return to normal, to bile and hate
For the public beast is at the gate.

Apple

I'm standing under a lamppost
Although the light is out
The darkness broken by the twilight
The quiet
By a shout.
When did the coldness close around us?
When did the decline begin?
Was it when Adam choose the apple?
Was it really such a sin?
Was love the rotten fruit,
Is passion the sword of doubt?
Jealousy and hunger
Envy in an eye
Lust the true destroyer
Revenge our apple pie.

Blood is on a flag
Which one belongs to you?
Which one holds your heart?
Which one is true for you?
One day the earth will rumble
One day the sky will fall
And some will say that apple
Was the ruin of us all.

Reflections

Come, sit you here and listen to the seagulls sing.
Is it not a haunting cry as it mingles with the ripples of the sea.
Each ripple a memory past, each gull's cry that doesn't last.
Does it speak to you of pleasant days, of love, laughter, tender sighs, the first hello's, the last goodbyes.
Memories so sweet that live in tears
Tears that hide
Memories revisited
Memories halted
Memories so cruel, best to be forgotten
Memories that make me whole and
Memories that tear me down again.
So, I sit, and I look out to sea
And think on things that used to be.
Old loves, old friends, and prayers that went unheeded
Childhood dreams I never needed.
Old age has brushed away old fears
And left me with these hidden tears.

Isolation song

Are you broken by shadows
Do the steps that you take have a price?
Your song is old and forgotten
And your thoughts have tarried too long.
Your hair is matted with confusion
And your dreams have somehow gone wrong.
You cling to your words with a passion
But your faith is broken and torn
You are lost
Like an old revolution
And your body is withered and worn.
You have lost your sense and your meaning
For a world that is passing you by
So, you sit and wait in the shadows
And join with the crows as they cry.

This face

This face has many features
Each one reassembled to form your point of view
So, gaze upon my features
And tell me what is new.
Am I the same as last year?
Do I fit your standard fare?
I'm that universal soldier
Do you wonder if I care?
I've had this face two thousand years
You've used it for your ends
Turned each loving brother
Into enemy, not friend.

I am used
This face is old
It's tired of its use.
This face with many features
Worn from man's abuse.
Come look upon me
And turn this face,
This face you use
And make it something new.

Feel the picture

I just can't feel the picture
Although its deep inside my head
Yet I know there's something out there
Is it something that I dread?

I stumble in the wilderness
Searching for the light
I try to make a picture
To help me through the night.
Two thousand years have passed
And my heart feels made of stone
Maybe that's why He walks in shadows
And why I walk alone.

They say He walks in shadows
For those who seek the light
So why do Angels hold the daytime
And Demons haunt the night.

My past remains well hidden
As my soul is kept from view
So, I'll walk amongst the shadows
Till I find what must be true.

A poor man walks in chains
A wise man lives in hope
A blind man lives in darkness
A seeing man lives to cope.

Pictures

Pictures at my window
Memories at my door
Dreams that chase my midnights
Confessors who ask for more.

Decades in embraces
Eons on our lips
Tears to greet the daylight
Magic in an eye
A hand that offers comfort
Paradise in a sigh.

Pictures of the past
Pictures still to come
Love and life a dreamer's tale
Stories of our making
Words that never fail.

Tread the path
Chase the demon dream
Race the stars to midnight
The Gods always hold a scheme.

Stand you true
And stand you fast
Winters wrath will soon to pass
Live the life
Like dreamer's do.

Those years

There was always violence in my youth
Those days of tumbling troubles
Those growing years.
A time of passage you say,
A time to prove my worth.
Where did it emerge from, this violence?
I never asked to be picked on
Yet I came to read the signs
I knew the time was 'now'
As the glee sat in their eyes.
That curling smile that betrayed other intentions.
I came to know the recurring anger
It came to me like an old friend
This anger, that walked by my side.
The stutter, those early years
A mind placed in self-isolation.
Of inward breath
The fear of speaking
The fear of anticipation to talk.
Such a common thing, to talk
Each day an endless walk.
Those years have passed
And fear subsides
Yet it sits there
Like a devil on my shoulder.
It no longer walks by my side
Just rest within, that anger
For once you have learnt it
It never leaves you truly alone.
You bury it, bury it deep.

Songs of NONSENSE

Time

Time...what is time?
You can't touch it
You can't smell it
You can't see it
It's not a tactile thing
Time for this
Time for that
Sometimes we don't have enough time
Sometimes we have too much time.
We say that time is precious
Yet we waste time.
Time on our hands
We even save time
And sometimes, time runs away with us.
We ask ourselves, "What have I done with my time?"
What time is it?
Have I got time?
Time is never your own
Yet it takes time to think about time
Well, time me out
Or time me in
I will always have time for you.

Power Man

I lay here now inside my bed
There's a picture I look at
As I look straight ahead.
A tattooed man
With arms of steel
Legs of iron
Full bodied
Moustachioed
Heavy with hair so black
That I imagine it runs all down his back.
White vest, black shorts
And written above the top of his head
Power Man, yes, Power Man, it must be said.
Yet there's humour here, just look at his eyes.
With bendy knees he looks at me
And one thing that I surmise is laughter,
The gift of fun
Which is no surprise.

A poem for today

I met a man upon my way, a happy man, I have to say.
I noticed as you do, he had three legs, not two!
A funny thought ran through my head so, this is what I went and said,
" *What do you do when you want socks! For socks they come in twos.*"
And this is what he said to me,
"*I swap them two to one and back to three, for this small task amuses me!*"
I thought this was a cunning plan coming from such a man.
He, with his three legs not two, for I suppose that's what you do. I asked if he would walk with me as I was going to the fair, a chance to meet some people there.
Some they stared with all their might, some they screamed and then took flight. He seemed unfazed, two legs or three, it was all the same to he. He didn't walk to the left, he didn't walk to the right, sometimes backwards...what a sight!
When he walked, motioned to the fore, he seemed to wander, Oh, I don't know, he didn't care which way he'd go.
But he looked the same as you and me, except of course, he's legs of three.
When he left me, he waved goodbye, shook my hand and what he said lingers still, inside my head.
"When I go, I think you'll find that previous notions you'll leave behind."
I think about him now and then and wonder if we'll meet again.
If you ever meet this man, who walks upon this sorry land with his legs of three not two, should it matter much to you?
He looks the same as you and me, except of course, his legs of three.

I ♥ ME

Vernon

Vernon, you see is a little like me
Yes, Vernon is a friend of mine.
Vernon, dear Vernon is a little like me.

Vernon and I would reach for the sky
And chase those clouds away.
Childhood friendships that would last forever
And then for an extra day.
Vernon, dear Vernon,
How we chased those clouds away.

Vernon had taken the habit of being a rabbit
Vernon hops and skips with childlike charm
And in his joy, I could find no harm.
For Vernon you see was never a winner
At lunch times or even at dinner.
Carrots and sprouts he would just spit them out
Shouting and screaming
He would really be dreaming
Of biscuits and ice cream
Of treacle tarts and custard
And strawberry jam on a thick slice of bread
All this deliciousness was inside his head.
With two button eyes of a different size
And a roughly stitched mouth that would stretch for a mile
Vernon, dear Vernon, with his roughly stitched smile.

Vernon and I would sit and talk of our dreams
Our hopes and fancy things.
Childish thoughts, pretending all day
Wondering what our dreams would bring
Yes, Vernon was a little like me.

He told me his wishes
Adventures he planned
The life he would lead
But dreams are like clouds
And time has blown them away
Like fairy dust
Consumed by the sky.

Time marches on and
Vernon has gone
Existing in the realm of make-believe.
A roughly stitched smile
Under two odd eyes of a different size.
Vernon was a dreamer
Yes, Vernon
Dear Vernon
He was a lot like me.

All Hallows

On a cold and cloudless night
when the moon stood still
and shone so bright
As I was walking to the harbour bound
I heard a sharp and curious sound.
Behind me came a man of clicks
A man so odd he walked on sticks.
He looked at me from underneath his tricorn hat
With eyes so sharp they cut the night
Like razor lines
A gaze so tight.
His face a sunken grey and ashen hue
My mind confused
What should I do?
My feet stuck firmly to the ground
While his
They made that clicking sound.

His long grey coat hung heavy
swaying neither left nor right
As he walked full front towards me
On that cold and frightful night.

He looked at me
and gave a sigh
Then clicked some more
And passed me by.
Rat's tails hung down
For hair like strands
And Spider-crabs made up his hands.

A spray of sea-mist brushed my face
As he increased his clicking pace.
Of my feet I found once more
For I followed on, down to the shore.
There amongst the seagull's cries
I spied a galleon in the bay
With tattered sails and creaking hull
A ghostly ship I saw that day.
He stood there as the waves rolled in
Two sticks planted in the sand
And spider-crabs made up his hands.
A misty swirl around him spread
With haunting voices of the dead
That filled the night inside my head.
He turned to me
His gaze so bright
Then disappeared
Into the night.

The old man of Dalkeith

There was an old man from Dalkeith
Who had an enormously large set of teeth.
It was often remarked, often said
That no one could see how they got in his head.
Never a gap to whistle a tune
And people remarked that he howled at the moon.
When he would smile
Infants would scream and run a full mile,
Parents would faint, dogs whimper away,
All this, all this, in the cold light of day.
For so large were his teeth
When the full moon did shine
The reflection of light
Could make you go blind.
His gait was stooped
For the weight of his teeth
Fastened his walk
Into a funny odd run
And he'd arrive at his destination
Before he'd begun.
When he passed away, the old man of Dalkeith
The tombstone was made using his teeth
Which they placed at the top
At the top of his head
The weight holding him down
To make sure he was dead.

Royal Snail

The post, it came late today, I cannot say why
Perhaps it's the rain, or did they try?
It's just like a bus, the mail, no letters day after day
And then all at once, it's three or it's four that comes rushing comes knocking to pour through your door.
Sometimes it goes to *God* knows where!
But I suppose *He* doesn't care
it matters not to *Him*, you see
If the post goes to you, or sometimes me.
I've bought a stamp, the letters gone
I don't know when or for how long.
It could be days
A month or more before it trickles through the front of your door.
Never fear, it will get there by pigeon post or maybe hare
come by van or train
that is of course...it doesn't rain.

The Old Witch of Blackheath

The old witch of Blackheath has terrible teeth,
their black and all wonky and she speaks with a lisp.
Her hair is matted and grey and her clothes are all dirty which
she wears every day.
There's a huge black wart that sits on the end of her nose and
her feet it's been said, don't smell like a rose.
Her toenails are green, their rather quite long and when she
breaks wind there's a terrible pong.
The old witch of Blackheath rides through the air
Looking down on poor mortals who don't really care.
She knows where she's going, she's been there before
Is she coming to your house?
Has she knocked on your door?
She'll cackle, she'll laugh, in her high-pitched tone
and when it goes quiet, who stands alone?
She throws out odd curses at those passing by
they just ignore her; they don't see her cry.
Some say she's not real, she's only a myth
Some say the old witch just takes the piss.
She wanders about in the sweet dead of night
She sleeps in odd openings she finds rather tight.
The old witch of Blackheath
She's a lady, for sure
A bag and some card
Does she need any more?

They found her, they say
In a doorway one day
No more, the old witch of Blackheath.

Write me a poem.

Write me a poem, you say
Do it now, do it today.
Do it now, do it fast
Write me poem with words that will last.
But poems are strange things
They wriggle and squirm
Their slippery creatures
Of that, I have learnt.
Poems that yell
Poems that scream
Poems of nightmares
Poems of dreams
Poems that sing
Poems with words that move all about
Poems are words
Some words last forever
Written with pen or the end of a feather.
Words that rhyme, words that chatter
Words with meaning
And words that don't really matter.
Write me a poem, you say.
Write me a poem, do it now, do it fast
But words are like clouds that drift through the sky
Some words say hello
Some words say goodbye.

Write me a poem
Write me a poem today
It's hard to write a poem
When you've nothing to say.

Mornings

Up in the morning
With a fart and a stretch
Look out through the window
And wonder what's next.
Down to my breakfast
And a nice cup of tea
Mornings are wonderful
Mornings are me.

Nonsense song

I was out and about going about what I was about when she followed me out looking about to see what I was about but I knew that whatever she was about was not what I was about trying to catch me out and the further out I got about I heard her shout but I was too far out getting about that why I went out I'd forgotten about!

Doorways

They laid him down inside a wooden box
Lid down fast
So, he wouldn't escape
A closet Houdini
Who left it too late

So much grief
So much sorrow
So many tears
For the no tomorrow.

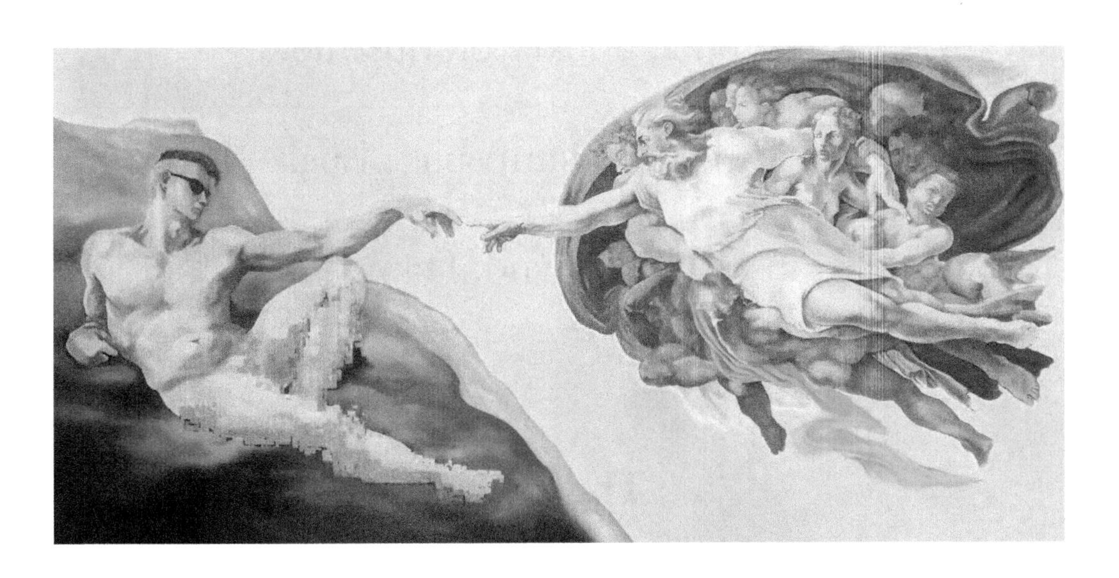

About the author

Lawrence Douglas Stephen Davis
Artist, poet, bricklayer, dreamer.

Born in Portsmouth, Hampshire, England, UK
1950.
Residing in Hayling Island, Hampshire, UK

The pen

The pen is such a humble tool
Wield it like a sword
And cut your words quite deep.

unused illustration for
ALL HALLOWS

Available on Amazon Books

Illustrations from INSIGHTS

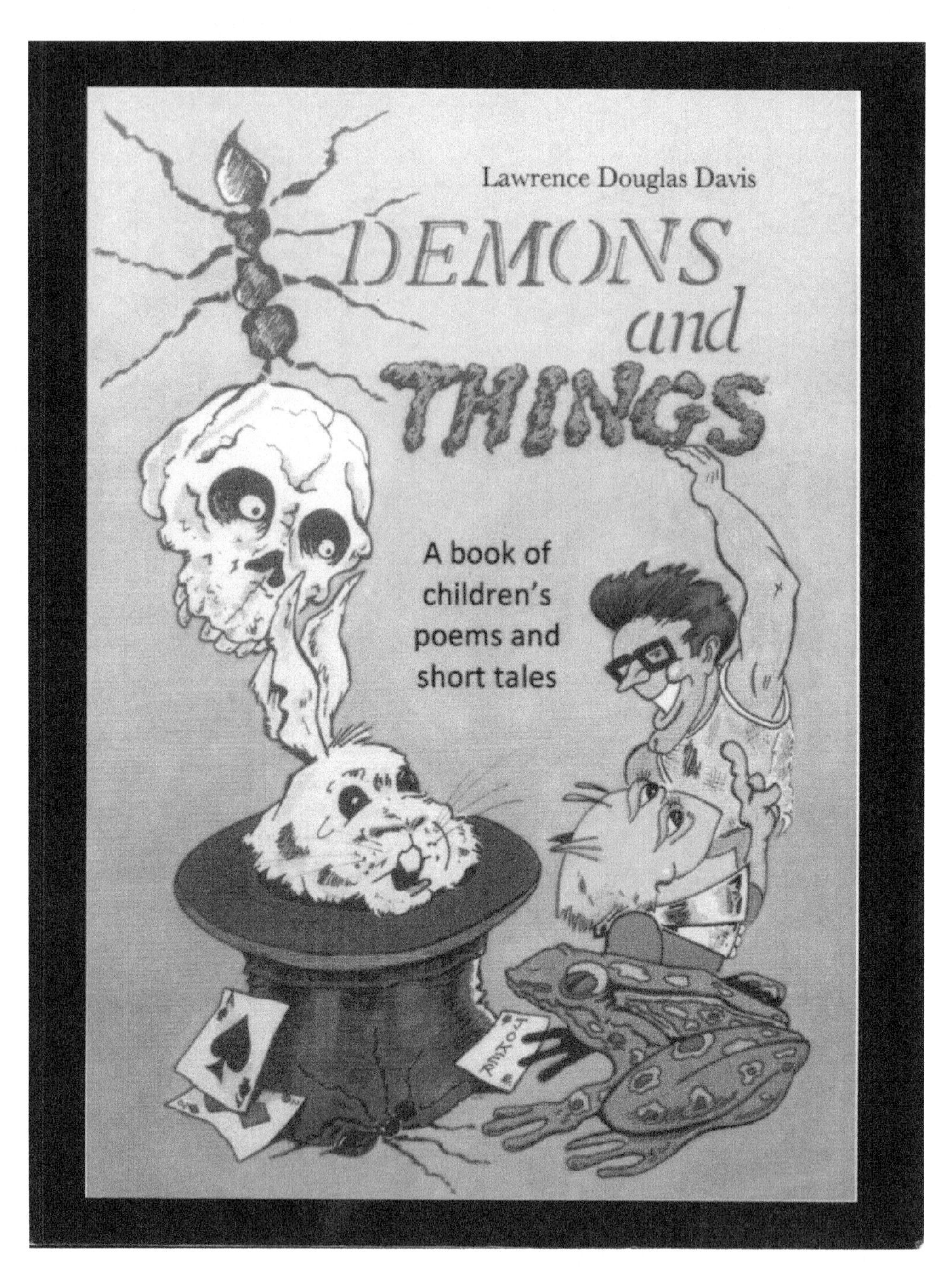

Available on Amazon Books

Illustrations from DEMONS and THINGS

Available on Amazon Books

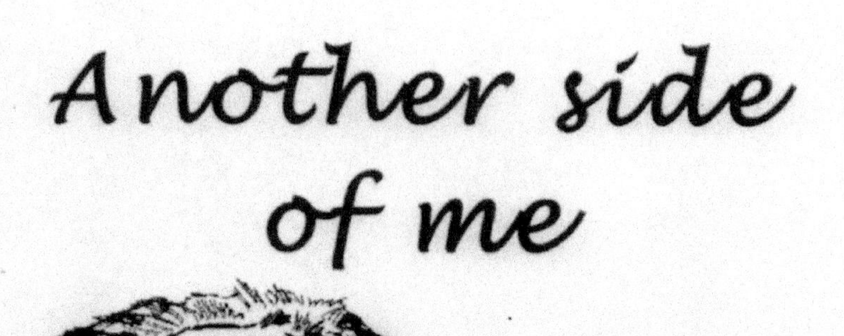

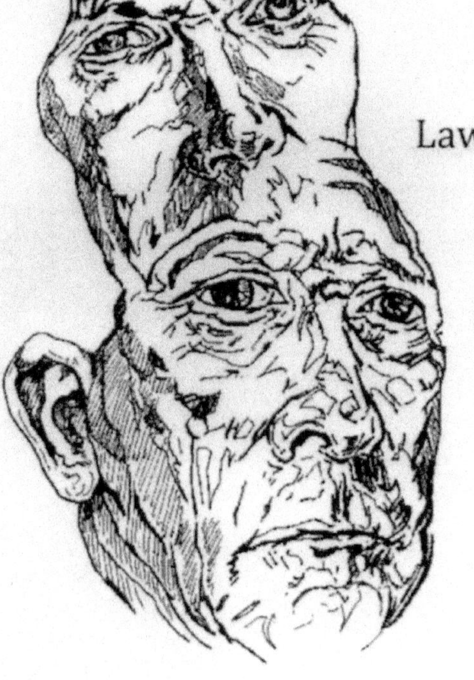

A selection of
poems

by

Lawrence Douglas
Davis

2023

Printed in Great Britain
by Amazon